FACTS ABOUT THE 50 STATES

← A FIRST BOOK →

FACTS ABOUT THE 50 STATES

By Sue R. Brandt

Maps by George Buctel

Illustrated with photographs

FRANKLIN WATTS | NEW YORK | LONDON

ACKNOWLEDGMENTS

For permission to use material from other sources, the author and publisher wish to express their gratitude to the following:

Material on the origin of state names (pages 20–25), names applied to state residents (pages 67–68), and abbreviations of state names (page 78) is used by permission from *Webster's Seventh New Collegiate Dictionary,* copyright 1967, and *Webster's Third New International Dictionary,* copyright 1966, by the G. & C. Merriam Company, publishers of the Merriam-Webster dictionaries.

The listing of official names of states, legislative bodies, and capitol buildings, which appears on pages 44–45, is reprinted with permission from *The Book of the States,* published every two years by the Council of State Governments.

The puzzle that appears on page 81 is reproduced through the courtesy of the American Can Company.

SBN 531-00687-5

Copyright © 1970 by Franklin Watts, Inc.
Library of Congress Catalog Card Number: 74-102276
Printed in the United States of America

10 9 8

For
Ronald, a Californian
Michael, a Coloradan
Charles, a New Yorker
Ginny Bel, Russell, and Roddy —
all Missourians

CONTENTS

LIST OF MAPS

FACTS ABOUT THE 50 STATES

NAMING THE STATES FROM MEMORY

Could you name the fifty states from memory? Most people probably could not. Yet it is not difficult to learn to do if you think of them in alphabetical order. There are ——

4 "A" states
  Alabama
  Alaska
  Arizona
  Arkansas

No "B" states

3 "C" states
  California
  Colorado
  Connecticut

1 "D" state
  Delaware

No "E" states

1 "F" state
  Florida

1 "G" state
  Georgia

1 "H" state
  Hawaii

4 "I" states
  Idaho
  Illinois
  Indiana
  Iowa

No "J" states

2 "K" states
  Kansas
  Kentucky

1 "L" state
  Louisiana

8 "M" states
  Maine
  Maryland
  Massachusetts
  Michigan
  Minnesota
  Mississippi
  Missouri
  Montana

8 "N" states
  (including 4 "News"
  and 2 "Norths")
  Nebraska
  Nevada

New Hampshire
New Jersey
New Mexico
New York
North Carolina
North Dakota

3 "O" states
  Ohio
  Oklahoma
  Oregon

1 "P" state
  Pennsylvania

No "Q" states

1 "R" state
  Rhode Island

2 "S" states
  South Carolina
  South Dakota

2 "T" states
  Tennessee
  Texas

1 "U" state
  Utah

2 "V" states
  Vermont
  Virginia

4 "W" states
  Washington
  West Virginia
  Wisconsin
  Wyoming

No "X," "Y," or
  "Z" states

(3)

CAN YOU RECOGNIZE THESE STATES?

The fifty states of the United States are somewhat like the members of a family. They are alike in some ways and different in others, as in size and shape. Can you recognize the states shown on the opposite page? Here are some clues:

COLORADO is an almost perfect rectangle. It is one of the few states with no boundaries formed by water.

MICHIGAN is made up of two parts. The lower part looks remarkably like a mitten.

OKLAHOMA is shaped like a stewpan, with a long, straight handle pointing to the west.

IDAHO resembles the side view of a throne, or a chair with a high back.

LOUISIANA looks like a boot with a ragged toe.

TENNESSEE is long from east to west. It resembles a sled, or maybe an anvil.

CONNECTICUT, third from the smallest state, is rectangular, except at the southwest corner.

WEST VIRGINIA has two parts called panhandles — one on the east and another on the north.

CALIFORNIA, third from the largest state, is shaped somewhat like a human arm, with a short upper arm and a long forearm bent toward the southeast.

MAINE looks somewhat like the head of a buffalo.

FLORIDA is long from north to south, with a panhandle pointing to the west.

MASSACHUSETTS ends in a "hook" in the east.

NEW JERSEY has about the same area as Massachusetts. But New Jersey is long and narrow, with zigzags on the west and the east.

ILLINOIS resembles an arrowhead, with part of one side broken off in a straight line.

DELAWARE, second smallest of all the states, has a northern boundary that is a perfect half circle. In shape, Delaware looks somewhat like Idaho, but Idaho is about forty times larger.

(4)

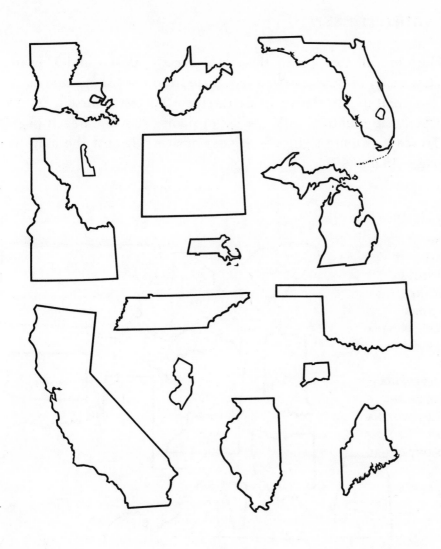

...AND THESE?

Here are all the rest of the states except Alaska and Hawaii. How many of them can you recognize from their shape and size? The capitals are shown as extra clues. To test yourself, try to match the numbers with the list of names shown on each page. To see if you are right, check your answers against the map on pages 48 and 49.

ALABAMA
INDIANA
KANSAS
MINNESOTA
MONTANA
NEW YORK
NORTH CAROLINA
NORTH DAKOTA
OHIO
PENNSYLVANIA
RHODE ISLAND
SOUTH CAROLINA
TEXAS
VERMONT

ARIZONA
ARKANSAS
GEORGIA
IOWA
KENTUCKY
MARYLAND
MISSISSIPPI
MISSOURI
NEBRASKA
NEVADA
NEW HAMPSHIRE
NEW MEXICO
OREGON
SOUTH DAKOTA
UTAH
VIRGINIA
WASHINGTON
WISCONSIN
WYOMING

1

2 ★ Little Rock

3 Cheyenne ★

★ Phoenix

5 ★ Jackson

6 Des Moines ★

4 ★ Salem

9 ★ Atlanta

★ Frankfort

7 ★ Salt Lake City

8

10 ★ Olympia

Richmond ★

15 ★ Carson City

13

11 ★ Pierre

12

14 Jefferson City ★

16 ★ Santa Fe

Madison ★

17 Annapolis ★

18 Concord ★

19 Lincoln ★

THE NEWEST MEMBERS OF THE FAMILY

Alaska is so large that if a map of it were drawn to the same scale as maps of the other states, it would need a whole page all for itself. For that reason it is not shown with the states on the preceding pages. Here is a drawing that will help you understand how Alaska compares in size with the conterminous United States.*

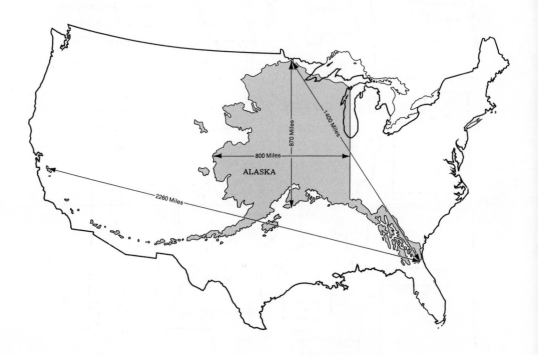

*The conterminous United States is the 48 states plus the District of Columbia, which made up the United States before Alaska gained statehood in 1959. The conterminous United States plus Alaska is called the continental United States.

(8)

If the islands that make up the state of Hawaii were drawn to the same scale as the other states, they would be so small that you could not tell very much about them. Here is a map that shows the sizes and shapes of the eight main islands. In addition, the state includes numerous scattered islets, reefs, and shoals.

Island	Nickname	Square Miles
Hawaii	The Big Island	4,021
Maui	The Valley Isle	728
Oahu	The Gathering Place	589
Kauai	The Garden Isle	551
Molokai	The Friendly Island	259
Lanai	The Pineapple Island	141
Niihau	The Mystery Island	72
Kahoolawe	(not inhabited)	45

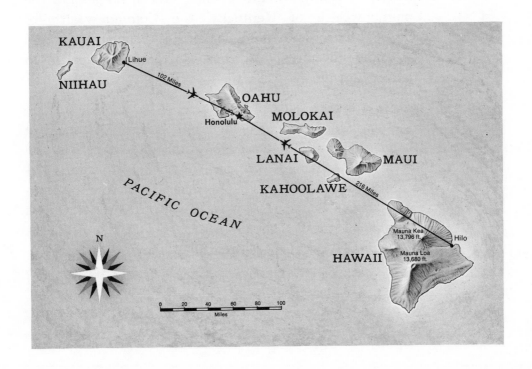

DO YOU KNOW...

Which of the fifty states has the longest name?
> Rhode Island, the smallest in land area, has the longest name. Its official name is the State of Rhode Island and Providence Plantations.

Which state has the shortest name?
> The names of Iowa, Ohio, and Utah are spelled with only four letters each. But Maine, with five letters, is the shortest to say. It is the only state name pronounced in only one syllable.

Which states do not call themselves states?
> Kentucky, Massachusetts, Pennsylvania, and Virginia call themselves commonwealths. Their official names are the Commonwealth of Kentucky, the Commonwealth of Massachusetts, the Commonwealth of Pennsylvania, and the Commonwealth of Virginia. But "commonwealth" in these names means the same as "state."

Which state was once a royal kingdom?
> In 1795, King Kamehameha I united most of the main islands of Hawaii into a kingdom that lasted for about one hundred years. King Kalakaua I, king of Hawaii from 1874 to 1891, wrote the words of the song that is now the state song, "Hawaii Ponoi" (Our Own Hawaii). His sister, Queen Liliuokalani, the last royal ruler of Hawaii, wrote the famous song "Aloha Oe" (Farewell to Thee).

Which state passed a law telling how its name should be spelled and pronounced?

(10)

King Kamehameha I, under whom a Hawaiian kingdom was formed in 1795.

Arkansas passed a law in 1881 declaring that its name is to be spelled A r k a n s a s (*not* A r k a n s a w) and pronounced ARK-un-saw (*not* Ar-KAN-zus).

Which state has the smallest number of people?

Alaska, the largest in land area, has the smallest population.

How Rhode Island, the smallest state, compares in size with Alaska, the largest state?

Alaska is almost 500 times larger than Rhode Island.

Which state lost first rank in number of people during the 1960's? Which state moved into first place?

New York lost first place to California.

Which states are surrounded by the greatest number of other states?

Missouri and Tennessee. Each is surrounded by eight other states.

(11)

Sand dunes in Death Valley, California, the lowest point in the United States. (SANTA FE RAILWAY)

Mount McKinley, in Alaska, at 20,320 feet, is the highest mountain in the United States. (UNITED PRESS INTERNATIONAL)

Where in the United States you could stand in four states all at once?

You could do this at the famous "Four Corners" of Utah, Colorado, New Mexico, and Arizona — the only place where the corners of four states touch.

Here are some other interesting "highests," "lowests," and "mosts" in the fifty states:

NORTHERNMOST POINT: Point Barrow, Alaska.

SOUTHERNMOST POINT: Ka Lae (South Cape), island of Hawaii (state of Hawaii).

EASTERNMOST POINT: West Quoddy Head, Maine.

WESTERNMOST POINT: Cape Wrangell, Attu Island (one of the Aleutian Islands), Alaska.

HIGHEST MOUNTAIN: Mount McKinley, Alaska (20,320 feet above sea level).

LOWEST POINT: Death Valley, California (282 feet below sea level).

HIGHEST TEMPERATURE EVER RECORDED: 134° Fahrenheit, in Inyo County (the Death Valley area), California.

(But temperatures of 100° F. or higher have been recorded in all the states.)

LOWEST TEMPERATURE EVER RECORDED: −76° F., at Tanana, Alaska; NEXT LOWEST: −70° F., at Rogers Pass, Montana.

(But all the states except Hawaii have recorded temperatures below zero.)

WETTEST PLACE: Mount Waialeale, on the island of Kauai (state of Hawaii), with an average yearly rainfall of 460 inches (more than 38 feet).

HOW THE UNITED STATES BEGAN — AND HOW IT GREW

The United States of America — also called the United States, the U.S.A., or sometimes "the States" — is a nation, or country, of the world. It takes its name from the fact that it is made up of states that are joined together, or united, by the Constitution to form one nation.

It began as thirteen colonies of England, spread out along the central Atlantic coast of North America. But the colonies did not come into being all at once. In fact, about 125 years passed between the founding of Virginia, the first colony, in 1607 and the founding of Georgia, the thirteenth, in 1733. More time passed — forty-three years — until the colonies joined together, rebelled against England, and declared on July 4, 1776, "That these United Colonies are, and of Right ought to be, Free and Independent States."

To gain freedom, the colonies fought the War of Independence, also called the Revolutionary War, or the American Revolution. The treaty of peace ending the war was signed in 1783. By this treaty England gave up its claim to the thirteen colonies, as well as to all land east of the Mississippi River from Canada to Florida.

The map on the opposite page shows when and how the United States added more land to its territory.

This map is from *The Statistical Abstract of the United States,* published each year by the Bureau of the Census, U.S. Department of Commerce, Washington, D.C.

THE BIRTHDAYS OF THE STATES

The date of the Declaration of Independence — July 4, 1776 — is the official "birthday" of the United States. Each of the original thirteen states might call July 4, 1776, its birthday, too.

Why, then, is Delaware sometimes called the first state, Pennsylvania the second, and so on?

To understand why, we need to know certain facts about the Constitution of the United States. After the War of Independence, the thirteen states were united under a form of government called the Articles of Confederation. But they soon realized that they needed a new and stronger form of national government.

In May, 1787, the states sent delegates, or representatives, to a meeting in Philadelphia called the Constitutional Convention. The delegates prepared a new form of government — the Constitution of the United States of America. They finished their work in September, 1787. Then a copy of the Constitution was sent to each of the thirteen states.

The people in each state chose delegates to study the Constitution and decide whether the state would ratify (approve) it. It was agreed that the Constitution would become the official form of government when nine of the thirteen states had voted to approve it. Delaware was the first to do so, and New Hampshire the ninth.

The following list shows the order in which the thirteen states ratified the Constitution:

    1st   Delaware — December 7, 1787
    2nd Pennsylvania — December 12, 1787
    3rd New Jersey — December 18, 1787

(16)

4th	Georgia — January 2, 1788
5th	Connecticut — January 9, 1788
6th	Massachusetts — February 6, 1788
7th	Maryland — April 28, 1788
8th	South Carolina — May 23, 1788
9th	New Hampshire — June 21, 1788
10th	Virginia — June 25, 1788
11th	New York — July 26, 1788
12th	North Carolina — November 21, 1789
13th	Rhode Island — May 29, 1790

The Constitution provided that new states might be admitted by the Congress of the United States. Before they gained statehood, most of the other thirty-seven states passed through a stage when they were known as territories of the United States. The territories were organized by Congress, and the chief officers were appointed by the President and the United States Senate. When the people in a territory felt that they were ready to form a state government, they would elect delegates to prepare a state constitution. Then they would vote to decide whether they would accept the constitution and ask to be admitted to the Union.

The list on pages 18 and 19 shows when the other states were organized as separate territories, when they were admitted to the Union (their official "birthdays"), and the order in which they were admitted. The notes that follow the list explain how states that were not organized as separate territories achieved statehood.

State	Organized as a Territory	Admitted to the Union	Order of Admission
Vermont		March 4, 1791	14th
Kentucky		June 1, 1792	15th
Tennessee		June 1, 1796	16th
Ohio		March 1, 1803	17th
Louisiana	1804	April 30, 1812	18th
Indiana	1800	December 11, 1816	19th
Mississippi	1798	December 10, 1817	20th
Illinois	1809	December 3, 1818	21st
Alabama	1817	December 14, 1819	22nd
Maine		March 15, 1820	23rd
Missouri	1812	August 10, 1821	24th
Arkansas	1819	June 15, 1836	25th
Michigan	1805	January 26, 1837	26th
Florida	1822	March 3, 1845	27th
Texas		December 29, 1845	28th
Iowa	1838	December 28, 1846	29th
Wisconsin	1836	May 29, 1848	30th
California		September 9, 1850	31st
Minnesota	1849	May 11, 1858	32nd
Oregon	1848	February 14, 1859	33rd
Kansas	1854	January 29, 1861	34th
West Virginia		June 20, 1863	35th
Nevada	1861	October 31, 1864	36th
Nebraska	1854	March 1, 1867	37th
Colorado	1861	August 1, 1876	38th
North Dakota	1861	November 2, 1889	39th*
South Dakota	1861	November 2, 1889	40th*
Montana	1864	November 8, 1889	41st

*When the official papers admitting North Dakota and South Dakota were signed, the names of the two states were covered so that no one would ever know which one was admitted first.

State	Organized as a Territory	Admitted to the Union	Order of Admission
Washington	1853	November 11, 1889	42nd
Idaho	1863	July 3, 1890	43rd
Wyoming	1868	July 10, 1890	44th
Utah	1850	January 4, 1896	45th
Oklahoma	1890	November 16, 1907	46th
New Mexico	1850	January 6, 1912	47th
Arizona	1863	February 14, 1912	48th
Alaska	1912	January 3, 1959	49th
Hawaii	1900	August 21, 1959	50th

Vermont was formed from lands claimed by both New Hampshire and New York. The dispute continued until 1777, when Vermont declared itself a free and independent republic. Finally the claims were settled, and Vermont became the fourteenth state.

Kentucky was part of Virginia until admitted as a state.

Before Tennessee became a state, it was first part of western North Carolina and then part of a large area known as the Territory South of the River Ohio.

Before Ohio became a state, it was part of a large area known as the Territory Northwest of the River Ohio.

Maine was part of Massachusetts until its admission to the Union as a separate state.

Texas was an independent country, known as the Republic of Texas, from 1836 until it was admitted as a state of the United States.

California prepared a constitution and used it to set up a government almost a year before it was admitted to the Union.

West Virginia was part of Virginia until admitted as a state.

HOW THE STATES RECEIVED THEIR NAMES

About half the states have names of Indian origin. The rest were named for persons or places or in various other interesting ways.

ALABAMA: Probably from Indian words *alba ayamule,* meaning "I make a clearing" (a clearing being a piece of land cleared of trees and brush).

ALASKA: From the Aleut word *alakshak,* meaning "peninsula."

ARIZONA: Probably from the Indian word *arizonac,* meaning "few springs," or "small springs."

ARKANSAS: From Indians, the Quapaws, meaning "downstream people"; they were called Arkansas by French explorers.

CALIFORNIA: Probably from the name of an imaginary island in a Spanish novel of about the year 1510. Explorers gave the name to the peninsula because they thought it resembled the imaginary island called California in the novel.

COLORADO: From the Spanish word *colorado,* meaning "red," or "reddish"; the name was first given to the river by early Spanish explorers to whom the waters looked reddish.

CONNECTICUT: Probably from Indian words *quinnitukq-ut,* meaning "at the long tidal river"; the name was first given to the Connecticut River, which is a tidal river, or river that flows into an ocean and is affected by the tides.

DELAWARE: From the Delaware River, named in honor of Lord Delaware (the title of Thomas West, also known as Baron De La Warr), one of the first governors of Virginia.

FLORIDA: From the Spanish words *Pascua florida*, meaning "flowery Easter." The name was chosen by the Spanish explorer Ponce de Leon because of the flowery appearance of the land and his discovery of it during the Easter season.

GEORGIA: For King George II of England, who granted the charter to the founders of the colony.

HAWAII: Possibly from *Havaiki*, which according to legend was the homeland of Polynesians who came from other islands and settled on the Hawaiian Islands.

IDAHO: Probably of Indian origin, although scholars have been unable to trace it in Indian languages.

ILLINOIS: From words in Indian languages meaning "man"; the French changed the words to Illinois.

INDIANA: From the word *Indian* plus the -a ending used in many geographical names.

IOWA: From the Indian word *Ayuhwa*, meaning literally "sleepy ones."

KANSAS: From *Kansa*, or *Kansas*, the name of a tribe of Indians who once lived in the area.

KENTUCKY: Probably related to the Indian word *kenta*, meaning "level" or "prairie," referring to the level land in the south-central part of the state.

LOUISIANA: Named Louisiane ("Land of Louis") in honor of Louis XIV, King of France.

MAINE: Probably named by French explorers in the 1500's for

Maine, an old region of France; called Maine by early New England fishermen to distinguish the main, or mainland, from the many islands along the coast.

MARYLAND: Named *Terra Mariae* (Latin words meaning "Land of Maria," or "Maryland") by King Charles I of England for his wife, Queen Henrietta Maria.

MASSACHUSETTS: From Massachusetts Bay, which was named for the Massachuset Indians, who lived around the Blue Hills near Boston; the name is made up of Indian words meaning "about the big hill."

MICHIGAN: From Lake Michigan, which takes its name from Indian words meaning "large lake."

MINNESOTA: From the Minnesota River, named from the Indian word *minisota,* meaning "white water."

MISSISSIPPI: From the Mississippi River, named from Indian words *misi,* meaning "big," and *sipi,* "river."

MISSOURI: From the Missouri River, which takes its name from an Indian people, the *Missouri,* meaning "owners of big canoes."

MONTANA: From the Latin word *montana,* meaning "mountainous regions."

NEBRASKA: From Indian words used as the early name of the Platte River. Later, the river received its present name, and the state received the Indian name.

NEVADA: Named for the Sierra Nevada, a mountain range on

the western border of the state. *Nevada* is Spanish for "snow-covered."

NEW HAMPSHIRE: Named for the county of Hampshire in England.

NEW JERSEY: Named for the island of Jersey, off the coast of England.

NEW MEXICO: Named for the country of Mexico.

NEW YORK: Named in honor of James, Duke of York and Albany, who received the land from his brother, King Charles II of England.

NORTH CAROLINA: From *Carolus,* the Latin form of the name Charles, in honor of King Charles I of England. (See SOUTH CAROLINA in this list.)

NORTH DAKOTA: From the *Dakota* Indians; the name means "allies."

OHIO: From the Ohio River, which probably was named from an Indian word, *oheo,* meaning "beautiful."

OKLAHOMA: From Indian words *okla humma,* or *okla homma,* meaning "red people."

OREGON: From Oregon River, an early name of the Columbia River.

PENNSYLVANIA: Named in honor of Sir William Penn, father of William Penn, the founder of Pennsylvania. The last part of the name (*-sylvania*) comes from the Latin word for "wood," or "forest."

RHODE ISLAND: The earliest settlements were called "plantations." The first one was named Providence by its founder, Roger Williams, "in commemoration of God's merciful providence." Later, the settlements of Portsmouth and Newport were incorporated with Providence under the name Providence Plantations. At the same time the largest island in Narragansett Bay, Aquidneck Island, was renamed Rhode Island, possibly after the Isle of Rhodes in the Aegean Sea. In 1663 the settlements adopted what is now the official name of the state — Rhode Island and Providence Plantations.

SOUTH CAROLINA: Same as North Carolina; the two Carolinas began as a single colony, which later was divided into a northern and a southern part.

SOUTH DAKOTA: Same as North Dakota; the Dakotas began as the territory of Dakota, which was divided into two parts.

TENNESSEE: From the Tennessee River, which was named for an Indian village called *Tanasi.*

TEXAS: From *techas,* an Indian word meaning "allies" or "friends."

UTAH: From *Yuta,* the name the Ute Indians called themselves.

VERMONT: From French words meaning "green mountains."

VIRGINIA: Named after Queen Elizabeth I of England, who was known as the Virgin Queen because she was unmarried.

WASHINGTON: Named for George Washington, the first President of the United States.

(24)

WEST VIRGINIA: So named because it originally was the western part of Virginia.

WISCONSIN: Probably from the Indian word *wishkonsing*, meaning "place of the beaver."

WYOMING: From Indian words meaning "on the great plain." The name was first given to the Wyoming Valley in eastern Pennsylvania.

A STATE CAPITAL QUIZ

Which state has the oldest capital?

New Mexico, one of the "youngest" states (the 47th), has the oldest capital. Its capital, SANTA FE, was founded by the Spanish as the capital of the province of New Mexico during the winter of 1609–10, and Santa Fe has been a seat of government ever since.

Is the capital of each state also the largest city in the state?

No, only these capitals are also their states' largest cities:

PHOENIX, Arizona
LITTLE ROCK, Arkansas
DENVER, Colorado
HARTFORD, Connecticut
ATLANTA, Georgia
HONOLULU, Hawaii
BOISE, Idaho
INDIANAPOLIS, Indiana
DES MOINES, Iowa

BOSTON, Massachusetts
JACKSON, Mississippi
OKLAHOMA CITY, Oklahoma
PROVIDENCE, Rhode Island
COLUMBIA, South Carolina
SALT LAKE CITY, Utah
CHARLESTON, West Virginia
CHEYENNE, Wyoming

How many capitals have the word "City" as part of their names?

Four — CARSON CITY, Nevada; OKLAHOMA CITY, Oklahoma; JEFFERSON CITY, Missouri; and SALT LAKE CITY, Utah.

Which capitals have names that end in *-polis* (the Greek word for "city")?

INDIANAPOLIS, Indiana, and ANNAPOLIS, Maryland.

Which capitals have names ending in *-ton* (a suffix meaning "village," or "town")?

TRENTON, New Jersey, and CHARLESTON, West Virginia.

Can you name all the state capitals from memory? If you cannot and would like to practice, turn to pages 79 and 80.

Des Moines is the capital and largest city of Iowa. (GREATER DES MOINES CHAMBER OF COMMERCE)

HOW THE STATE CAPITALS WERE NAMED

Almost half of the state capitals were named in honor of persons. Several were named for other cities or towns, two were named for their states, and some have Indian, French, or Spanish names. Others were named in various ways.

How many capitals were named for Christopher Columbus?

Two — COLUMBUS, Ohio, and COLUMBIA, South Carolina.

Which capitals have names honoring Presidents of the United States?

JACKSON, Mississippi, for President Andrew Jackson.

JEFFERSON CITY, Missouri, for President Thomas Jefferson.

LINCOLN, Nebraska, for President Abraham Lincoln.

MADISON, Wisconsin, for President James Madison.

What other capitals were named for persons?

MONTGOMERY, Alabama: For General Richard Montgomery, a hero of the Revolutionary War.

JUNEAU, Alaska: For Joe Juneau, one of the prospectors who found gold in the area in 1880.

DENVER, Colorado: For James William Denver, governor in 1858 of Kansas Territory, of which Colorado then was a part.

FRANKFORT, Kentucky: First called Frank's Ford for a pioneer, Stephen Frank, who had been killed by Indians at a ford (river crossing) in the Kentucky River; later named Frankfort.

AUGUSTA, Maine: Probably for Pamela Augusta Dearborn,

daughter of Henry Dearborn, a Revolutionary War general.

ANNAPOLIS, Maryland: For Queen Anne of England.

SAINT PAUL, Minnesota: For Saint Paul, to whom in 1841 Father Lucien Galtier dedicated a log church, around which a settlement, also called Saint Paul, grew.

CARSON CITY, Nevada: For Christopher (Kit) Carson, Indian scout and frontiersman.

TRENTON, New Jersey: For William Trent, a Philadelphia businessman who laid out the town.

ALBANY, New York: For James, Duke of York and Albany (later King James II of England).

RALEIGH, North Carolina: For Sir Walter Raleigh.

BISMARCK, North Dakota: For the German statesman Bismarck.

Abraham Lincoln (left) and Andrew Jackson (right) are two United States Presidents for whom state capitals were named.

HARRISBURG, Pennsylvania: For John Harris, who established a trading post at the site.

PIERRE, South Dakota: For Pierre Chouteau, a member of the Chouteau family, who helped to found St. Louis, Missouri, and who later made a great fortune trading with the Indians.

NASHVILLE, Tennessee: For Francis Nash, Revolutionary War general.

AUSTIN, Texas: For Stephen F. Austin, a leader in Texas' struggle for independence from Mexico.

CHARLESTON, West Virginia: For Charles Clendenin; named by his son Colonel George Clendenin, a Revolutionary War soldier and owner of the land on which the settlement was built.

Which capitals were named for their states?

INDIANAPOLIS, Indiana, and OKLAHOMA CITY, Oklahoma.

How many capitals were named for cities or towns in England?

Four — HARTFORD, Connecticut; DOVER, Delaware; BOSTON, Massachusetts; and RICHMOND, Virginia.

Which capitals were named for other cities or towns?

LANSING, Michigan: For Lansing, a village in New York, from which some of the first settlers came.

HELENA, Montana: For Helena, Minnesota, former home of an early settler.

MONTPELIER, Vermont: Probably from the city of Montpellier, France.

Which capitals take their name from physical features?

LITTLE ROCK, Arkansas: From a rocky formation on the

bank of the Arkansas River called "Little Rock" to distinguish it from a larger rocky bluff up the river.

SPRINGFIELD, Illinois: Probably from a creek called Spring Creek on land where the settlement was built.

SALT LAKE CITY, Utah: From Great Salt Lake.

OLYMPIA, Washington: From the Olympic Mountains, northwest of the city.

Which capitals have Indian, French, or Spanish names?

SACRAMENTO, California: From *Sacramento,* a Spanish word meaning "the Blessed Sacrament."

TALLAHASSEE, Florida: From an Indian word meaning "old field," or "old town."

BOISE, Idaho: Named by French Canadians who, after journeying through treeless country, are said to have exclaimed *"Les Bois!"* ("The woods!" or "The trees!") when they saw trees in the vicinity of the present city.

The Great Salt Lake in Utah gave its name to the state's capital, Salt Lake City. The railroad bridge shown here is seldom used today. (CHARLES PHELPS CUSHING)

The Olympic Mountains, which gave their name to Olympia, Washington, are part of a wild and beautiful area of the United States. (UNITED PRESS INTERNATIONAL)

DES MOINES, Iowa: From the Des Moines River, which was probably named for an Indian tribe called Moingouena. French explorers called the river Rivière des Moingouenas, and then by a shortened form, Rivière des Moings. Later the name was written Des Moines (*moine* meaning "monk" in French) because monks once had lived in huts along the riverbank and people thought the name was meant to be "river of the monks."

TOPEKA, Kansas: From an Indian word meaning "a good place to dig potatoes, or roots."

BATON ROUGE, Louisiana: From a red post, or stick, that was used to mark the boundary between the hunting grounds of two Indian tribes; early French explorers used the words *baton rouge* (French for "red post, or stick") as the name of the place.

SANTA FE, New Mexico: A shortened form of the original Spanish name *La Villa Real de la Santa Fe de San Francisco de Asis* ("The Royal City of the Holy Faith of Saint Francis of Assisi").

CHEYENNE, Wyoming: For the Cheyenne Indians.

Which capitals were named for an idea?

CONCORD, New Hampshire: For the idea of concord (meaning "state of agreement, or harmony").

SALEM, Oregon: From the Hebrew word *shalom* (which is used as a greeting and which means "well-being," or "peace").

PROVIDENCE, Rhode Island: Named in commemoration of "God's merciful providence" ("providence" meaning "divine guidance, or care").

And how did the rest of the capitals get their names?

PHOENIX, Arizona: From the mythical bird, the phoenix. Early settlers founded the city in the 1860's on lands where the prehistoric Hohokam Indians had built irrigation canals to water their crops. The settlers rebuilt some of the canals and predicted that a new city would arise "phoenixlike" where ancient Indian pueblos once stood. (According to mythology, the phoenix caused itself to be destroyed by fire and then arose from its ashes more beautiful and youthful than ever before.)

ATLANTA, Georgia: From the word "Atlantic" in the name of the Western and Atlantic Railroad; the city was the southeastern terminus of the railroad.

HONOLULU, Hawaii: The name is Hawaiian for "sheltered bay."

THE AREA OF THE STATES

Large land areas, such as the areas of the states, are measured in square miles. It is difficult to imagine the size of the states, but it is helpful to know what "square mile" means. A square piece of land one mile long and one mile wide has an area of one square mile.

On the opposite page, the states are arranged according to area in square miles. They are in groups of ten, with the ten largest first, and so on. When they are grouped in this way, you can tell something about how they compare in area, and you can discover some interesting facts. For example, quite a few of the states have about the same area. Could you have guessed which ones these are simply by looking at a map of the United States? Here are some questions that you might try to answer:

Which states would you name as having nearly the same area?

About how many square miles does a medium-sized state cover?

Are all the twenty largest states east of the Mississippi River or west of that river?

Which is the largest state east of the Mississippi?

One group of states is known as the New England states. These are Maine, Massachusetts, New Hampshire, Vermont, Connecticut, and Rhode Island. Which one of these is the largest?

How many states are larger in area than all the New England states put together?

Which one of the Dakotas is the larger? Which one of the Carolinas?

(34)

		SQ. MI.*			SQ. MI.
1st	Alaska	586,412	11th	Utah	84,916
2nd	Texas	267,339	12th	Minnesota	84,068
3rd	California	158,693	13th	Idaho	83,557
4th	Montana	147,138	14th	Kansas	82,264
5th	New Mexico	121,666	15th	Nebraska	77,227
6th	Arizona	113,909	16th	South Dakota	77,047
7th	Nevada	110,540	17th	North Dakota	70,665
8th	Colorado	104,247	18th	Oklahoma	69,919
9th	Wyoming	97,914	19th	Missouri	69,686
10th	Oregon	96,981	20th	Washington	68,192

		SQ. MI.			SQ. MI.
21st	Georgia	58,876	31st	Louisiana	48,523
22nd	Florida	58,560	32nd	Mississippi	47,716
23rd	Michigan	58,216	33rd	Pennsylvania	45,333
24th	Illinois	56,400	34th	Tennessee	42,244
25th	Iowa	56,290	35th	Ohio	41,222
26th	Wisconsin	56,154	36th	Virginia	40,817
27th	Arkansas	53,104	37th	Kentucky	40,395
28th	North Carolina	52,586	38th	Indiana	36,291
29th	Alabama	51,609	39th	Maine	33,215
30th	New York	49,576	40th	South Carolina	31,055

		SQ. MI.
41st	West Virginia	24,181
42nd	Maryland	10,577
43rd	Vermont	9,609
44th	New Hampshire	9,304
45th	Massachusetts	8,257
46th	New Jersey	7,836
47th	Hawaii	6,450
48th	Connecticut	5,009
49th	Delaware	2,057
50th	Rhode Island	1,214

The total area of the United States is 3,615,123 square miles. This includes 67 square miles occupied by the District of Columbia (see page 40).

*All the area figures on this page are from *The Statistical Abstract of the United States.*

(35)

THE POPULATION

In what way was November 20, 1967, an important date in the history of the United States?

At 11:00 A.M. on that date, a mechanism in Washington, D.C., called the Census Clock, showed that the population of the United States had reached 200 million. A photograph of the Census Clock appears on the opposite page.

In what year did the population reach 100 million?

It reached that number in 1915.

How many years did it take the nation to reach its first 100 million?

It took 308 years (from 1607 until 1915).

How many years did it take the United States to reach the second 100 million?

Only 52 years (from 1915 until 1967).

When do scientists expect the population to reach 300 million?

About the year 2000.

Does the Census Clock give an exact count of the population?

No, but it is as accurate as scientists can make it. They set the dials on the clock according to recent average number of births, number of deaths, and number of persons leaving and entering the country. The mechanism of the clock balances all these figures and shows the net gain. A dial keeps track of the ever-changing total number. The clock is only one of various ways of estimating the population (judging what the population may be) between the years when an official count is made.

(36)

The constantly changing population of the United States is estimated on the Census Clock. (THE UNITED STATES DEPARTMENT OF COMMERCE)

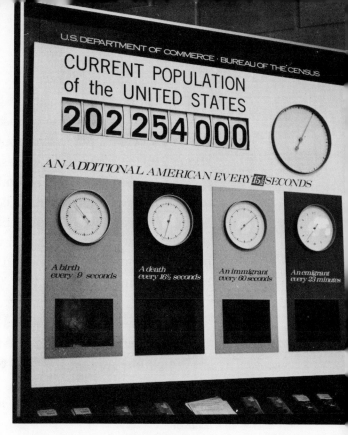

How is the most exact count possible made?

The United States Bureau of the Census makes a count, called the census. The first census was taken in 1790, and there has been an official census every ten years since then — in 1800, 1810, 1820, and so on. The following table shows how the population of the United States has increased from time to time:

Census Year	Population	Census Year	Population
1790	3,929,214	1900	75,994,575
1800	5,308,483	1950	150,697,361
1850	23,191,876	1970	203,235,298

The list on the opposite page shows each state's population (rounded to the nearest thousand) and its rank at the time of the 1970 census, when the population of the whole country was about 203,235,298. The states are listed in groups of ten, with the ten largest first, and so on. This arrangement makes it easy for you to see how each state compares with the others in population. You can also tell something about the parts of the country that have the most people, and you can compare each state's rank in population with its rank in area (see the list on page 35). Here are some questions that you might answer:

Which ones of the ten states that are largest in population are located along (or near) the Atlantic coast?

Which one among the first ten in population is along the Pacific coast?

Which ones of the first ten in population are along the Great Lakes?

How many of the states that rank from 11th to 20th in population are along the Atlantic coast (including the Gulf of Mexico) or along the Great Lakes?

States that are medium-sized in population have about how many people?

Which states are among the first ten both in population and in area?

Which ones are among the first ten in population but among the last ten in area?

Which states are among the last ten both in population and in area?

The District of Columbia had about 809,000 people. Where would it rank if it were placed in the list with the states?

		POPULATION*				POPULATION*
1st	California	19,953,000	11th	Indiana		5,194,000
2nd	New York	18,241,000	12th	North Carolina		5,082,000
3rd	Pennsylvania	11,794,000	13th	Missouri		4,677,000
4th	Texas	11,197,000	14th	Virginia		4,648,000
5th	Illinois	11,114,000	15th	Georgia		4,590,000
6th	Ohio	10,652,000	16th	Wisconsin		4,418,000
7th	Michigan	8,875,000	17th	Tennessee		3,924,000
8th	New Jersey	7,168,000	18th	Maryland		3,922,000
9th	Florida	6,789,000	19th	Minnesota		3,805,000
10th	Massachusetts	5,689,000	20th	Louisiana		3,643,000

		POPULATION*				POPULATION*
21st	Alabama	3,444,000	31st	Oregon		2,091,000
22nd	Washington	3,409,000	32nd	Arkansas		1,923,000
23rd	Kentucky	3,219,000	33rd	Arizona		1,772,000
24th	Connecticut	3,032,000	34th	West Virginia		1,744,000
25th	Iowa	2,825,000	35th	Nebraska		1,484,000
26th	South Carolina	2,591,000	36th	Utah		1,059,000
27th	Oklahoma	2,559,000	37th	New Mexico		1,016,000
28th	Kansas	2,249,000	38th	Maine		994,000
29th	Mississippi	2,217,000	39th	Rhode Island		950,000
30th	Colorado	2,207,000	40th	Hawaii		770,000

		POPULATION*
41st	New Hampshire	738,000
42nd	Idaho	713,000
43rd	Montana	694,000
44th	South Dakota	666,000
45th	North Dakota	618,000
46th	Delaware	548,000
47th	Nevada	489,000
48th	Vermont	445,000
49th	Wyoming	332,000
50th	Alaska	302,000

*You will understand that population figures are always changing. As a state gains or loses in population, it may move up or down in rank. To find the population of each state and its rank before the last census, look in *The Statistical Abstract of the United States* or in an almanac such as *The World Almanac and Book of Facts*. New editions of these books are published each year, and they give many interesting facts about population.

(39)

THE DISTRICT OF COLUMBIA

The initials "D.C." in the name of the national capital, Washington, D.C., stand for "District of Columbia." The District is situated on the Potomac River, on land that once was part of the state of Maryland. Because the city of Washington covers the whole area, the names "Washington, D.C." and "District of Columbia" actually have the same meaning.

In the beginning, the District of Columbia included 100 square miles (an area 10 miles wide and 10 miles long) given to the federal government by Maryland and Virginia in 1791. But the part given by Virginia was returned to that state in 1846. The total area at present is 67 square miles (61 square miles of land and 6 square miles of water).

The District is a federal district (a special area set apart as the seat of the United States Government), not a state or a part

(40)

of any state, and it is governed by special rules. It has no representatives in the Congress of the United States. The Twenty-third Amendment to the Constitution gave the citizens of the District the right to vote in Presidential elections. But they did not have this right until the amendment was approved in 1961.

Through the years the District of Columbia has had various forms of local government. Under a new plan started in 1967, the government has two branches. The executive branch is made up of a commissioner (also called a "mayor") and an assistant to the commissioner. Both are appointed by the President of the United States. The legislative branch is called the District of Columbia Council. It has nine members, all appointed by the President.

The Capitol dome, seen through the trees, is only one of many beautiful sights in Washington, D.C. (UNITED PRESS INTERNATIONAL)

HOW THE STATES ARE GOVERNED

All the states have about the same form of government. All have constitutions, much like the Constitution of the United States, which divide the powers of government into three branches.

The legislative branch legislates (makes the laws).

The executive branch executes (carries out) the laws.

The judicial branch, which is made up of a system of courts, judges questions about the laws.

The head of the executive branch of the national government is the President. The head in each state is the governor.

The legislative branch of the national government is the Congress of the United States. It is made up of two bodies, or chambers, called the Senate and the House of Representatives. In all the states except one (Nebraska), the legislative branch also is made up of two bodies.

All the states call this branch by the general name "legislature," and about half of them use "Legislature" as the official name. The table on pages 44-45 gives the official name used in each state.

Nebraska has a unicameral legislature — that is, a legislature of only one body, or chamber. All the other states, like the national government, have bicameral law-making bodies. (The prefix *uni-* means "one," and the prefix *bi-* means "two.") As the table shows, all of the states call one body the Senate and most of them call the second body the House of Representatives.

(42)

Each state, like the nation, has a capital and a capitol. These words sometimes are confused, but they should not be.

Capital (spelled with *-tal* as the last syllable) means "city that is the seat of government."

Capitol (spelled with *-tol* as the last syllable) means "the building where the legislative branch of government meets."

In most states — but not all — the official name of the capitol is "State Capitol." Most of the capitols are stately buildings with domes, somewhat like the Capitol of the United States in the national capital, Washington, D.C.

The State Capitol in Madison, Wisconsin (left), is a traditional, domed building. The Louisiana State Capitol at Baton Rouge (right) is a thirty-four-story skyscraper. (CHARLES PHELPS CUSHING)

OFFICIAL NAMES OF STATES, LEGISLATIVE BODIES, AND CAPITOL BUILDINGS*

State	Both bodies	Senate	House	Capitol building
Alabama, State of	Legislature	Senate	House of Representatives	State Capitol
Alaska, State of	Legislature	Senate	House of Representatives	State Capitol
Arizona, State of	Legislature	Senate	House of Representatives	State Capitol
Arkansas, State of	General Assembly	Senate	House of Representatives	State Capitol
California, State of	Legislature	Senate	Assembly	State Capitol
Colorado, State of	General Assembly	Senate	House of Representatives	State Capitol
Connecticut, State of	General Assembly	Senate	House of Representatives	State Capitol
Delaware, State of	General Assembly	Senate	House of Representatives	Legislative Hall
Florida, State of	Legislature	Senate	House of Representatives	State Capitol
Georgia, State of	General Assembly	Senate	House of Representatives	State Capitol
Hawaii, State of	Legislature	Senate	House of Representatives	State Capitol
Idaho, State of	Legislature	Senate	House of Representatives	State Capitol
Illinois, State of	General Assembly	Senate	House of Representatives	State House
Indiana, State of	General Assembly	Senate	House of Representatives	(a)
Iowa, State of	General Assembly	Senate	House of Representatives	State Capitol
Kansas, State of	Legislature	Senate	House of Representatives	State House(b)
Kentucky, Commonwealth of .	General Assembly	Senate	House of Representatives	State Capitol
Louisiana, State of	Legislature	Senate	House of Representatives	State Capitol
Maine, State of	Legislature	Senate	House of Representatives	State House
Maryland, State of	General Assembly	Senate	House of Delegates	State House
Massachusetts, Common-wealth of	General Court	Senate	House of Representatives	State House
Michigan, State of	Legislature	Senate	House of Representatives	State Capitol
Minnesota, State of	Legislature	Senate	House of Representatives	State Capitol
Mississippi, State of	Legislature	Senate	House of Representatives	State Capitol
Missouri, State of	General Assembly	Senate	House of Representatives	State Capitol
Montana, State of	Legislative Assembly	Senate	House of Representatives	State Capitol
Nebraska, State of	Legislature	Unicameral		State Capitol

*From *The Book of the States*, published by the Council of State Governments.

(44)

State	Legislature	Upper House	Lower House	Building
Nevada, State of	Legislature	Senate	Assembly	State Capitol
New Hampshire, State of	General Court	Senate	House of Representatives	State House
New Jersey, State of	Legislature	Senate	General Assembly	State House
New Mexico, State of	Legislature	Senate	House of Representatives	State Capitol
New York, State of	Legislature	Senate	Assembly	State Capitol
North Carolina, State of	General Assembly	Senate	House of Representatives	State Capitol(c)
North Dakota, State of	Legislative Assembly	Senate	House of Representatives	State Capitol
Ohio, State of	General Assembly	Senate	House of Representatives	State House(b)
Oklahoma, State of	Legislature	Senate	House of Representatives	State Capitol
Oregon, State of	Legislative Assembly	Senate	House of Representatives	State Capitol
Pennsylvania, Commonwealth of	General Assembly	Senate	House of Representatives	Capitol Building
Rhode Island and Providence Plantations, State of	General Assembly	Senate	House of Representatives	State House
South Carolina, State of	General Assembly	Senate	House of Representatives	State House
South Dakota, State of	Legislature	Senate	House of Representatives	State Capitol
Tennessee, State of	General Assembly	Senate	House of Representatives	State Capitol
Texas, State of	Legislature	Senate	House of Representatives	State Capitol(b)
Utah, State of	Legislature	Senate	House of Representatives	State Capitol
Vermont, State of	General Assembly	Senate	House of Representatives	State House
Virginia, Commonwealth of ...	General Assembly	Senate	House of Delegates	State Capitol
Washington, State of	Legislature	Senate	House of Representatives	Legislative Building
West Virginia, State of	Legislature	Senate	House of Delegates	State Capitol
Wisconsin, State of	Legislature	Senate	Assembly	State Capitol
Wyoming, State of	Legislature	Senate	House of Representatives	State Capitol

(a) No official name. Both "State House" and "State Capitol" used.

(b) Unofficial.

(c) Since 1963, the legislature has met in its own building, "Legislative Building."

THE GEOGRAPHY OF THE STATES

What are the main physical features of the United States?
We might think of three main features. These are two great mountain systems — the Appalachians in the east and the Rockies in the west — with a broad central lowland stretching out between them.

How do the Appalachians and the Rockies compare in size?
The Rockies are more than twice as high as the Appalachians. The highest peak in the Rockies, Mount Elbert in Colorado, is 14,431 feet above sea level. The highest peak in the Appalachians, Mount Mitchell in North Carolina, is 6,684 feet.

The Rockies are much longer. They extend from New Mexico to the Canadian border, continue through Canada, and then turn westward into Alaska. The Appalachians extend from Alabama to Maine.

The Rockies are also much broader. They take up about one third of all the area of the conterminous United States.

What is the Continental Divide?
The line formed by the highest peaks of the Rockies is called by this name because it divides the continent. Rivers that begin on the western side of the Rockies flow generally toward the western side of the continent, and rivers rising on the eastern side flow generally eastward.

How large is the lowland between the Appalachians and the Rockies?

(46)

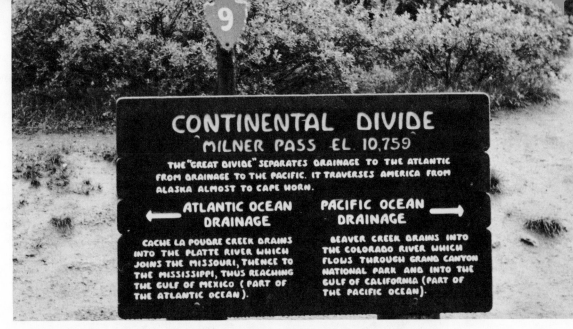

A marker at Milner Pass in Rocky Mountain National Park, in Colorado, identifies the Continental Divide. (PHOTO BY BEN ROTHSTEIN FROM CUSHING)

It is about 1,500 miles from east to west, and it covers half the conterminous United States.

Is this lowland really low in elevation?

Some parts are, and others are not. But the whole region is low in comparison with the mountain ribs on either side.

What other names are given to the central lowland, or parts of it?

Other names are "plains" and "prairie," meaning "broad stretches of level and almost treeless country." But many parts are neither level nor treeless, except in comparison with the rugged and heavily forested mountain systems. The highest (western) part is called the Great Plains.

(47)

THE UNITED STATES

A D A

MINNESOTA

Lake Superior

Lake Huron

Lake Michigan

MICHIGAN

WISCONSIN

Duluth
Sault Ste. Marie

St. Paul
Minneapolis

Madison
Milwaukee

Grand Rapids
Flint
Lansing

IOWA
Davenport
Des Moines
Peoria
ILLINOIS
Springfield

Sioux City
Sioux Falls

Chicago
Gary

INDIANA
Indianapolis

Detroit
Cleveland

Lake Erie

Toronto
Lake Ontario
Buffalo

NEW YORK

Quebec

Montreal
St. Lawrence River

Ottawa

MAINE
Augusta

VT
Montpelier
N.H.
Concord
Portland

MASS.
Boston
Albany
Hartford
Providence
CONN. R.I.

New York

N.J.
Trenton
Philadelphia

HIGHLANDS

PENNSYLVANIA
Pittsburgh
Harrisburg

OHIO
Columbus
Cincinnati

WEST
VIRGINIA
Charleston

Baltimore
Washington, D.C.
Annapolis
MD.
DEL.
Dover

Mississippi River
Missouri River

maha
Lincoln

Kansas City
Topeka
Wichita

Kansas City
Jefferson City
St. Louis

MISSOURI

Louisville
Lexington

Frankfort

KENTUCKY

Ohio River

VIRGINIA
Richmond
Norfolk

Mt. Mitchell 6,684 ft.

NORTH CAROLINA
Raleigh
Charlotte

Tulsa
Oklahoma City
OKLAHOMA
Ft. Smith
Little Rock

ARKANSAS
Memphis

Arkansas R.

Nashville
TENNESSEE

Tennessee R.

APPALACHIAN

SOUTH CAROLINA
Columbia
Charleston

Dallas
ort Worth
Shreveport
LOUISIANA

Jackson
MISSISSIPPI

Birmingham

ALABAMA

Montgomery

Atlanta
GEORGIA
Savannah

Mississippi River

Baton Rouge
Mobile
Tallahassee

Jacksonville

Austin
Houston
Galveston
New Orleans

Cape Kennedy

Tampa
FLORIDA

Miami

GULF OF MEXICO

ATLANTIC OCEAN

Red River of the North

Red River

STRAITS OF FLORIDA

TROPIC OF CANCER

Havana
CUBA

0 200 400 600 800
Miles

50°N
45°N
40°N
35°N
30°N
25°N

95°W 90°W 85°W 80°W 75°W 70°W 65°W

Of course, there are many features in the United States besides two mountain ribs and a central lowland. For example, there is yet another mountain rib west of the Rocky Mountains. What is it?

The third main mountain rib is made up of the Sierra Nevada (mountains chiefly in western California) and the Cascade Range, which joins the Sierra Nevada on the north and continues through Oregon and Washington. Mount Whitney (14,494 feet) in the Sierra Nevada is higher than any of the peaks of the Rockies. Until Alaska joined the Union, it was the highest peak in the United States.

The name Sierra Nevada is Spanish for "snowy mountain range." If we know the meaning, we will understand why the word "mountains" is not added to the name Sierra Nevada. In somewhat the same way, we do not add "river" to the name Rio Grande because *rio* is the Spanish word for "river."

What are coastal plains?

The lowlands bordering the coasts are called by this name. The Atlantic Coastal Plain extends from Cape Cod (Massachusetts) and Long Island (New York) all the way to Florida. There it joins the Gulf Coastal Plain, which continues across the states along the Gulf of Mexico. The coastal plains bordering the Pacific coast are generally much narrower than the other coastal plains.

What is the Piedmont?

Piedmont (from Piedmont, in Italy) is a name for lands lying at the base of mountains. In the United States, this

(50)

name usually is given to the region between the Appalachians and the Atlantic Coastal Plain.

Which state has the highest mountains of all?

Alaska has that distinction. The mountains of southern Alaska have at least fifteen peaks that are higher than Mount Whitney. Mount McKinley, in the Alaska Range of south-central Alaska, is 20,320 feet above sea level. It is the highest peak in all of North America.

A view of the Alaska Range in Mount McKinley National Park. (PHOTO BY SAWDERS FROM CUSHING)

Mauna Kea, Hawaii's tallest mountain, rises to 13,796 feet above sea level.
(PHOTO BY R. WENKAM)

How do the mountains of Hawaii compare with mountains in the other states?

Hawaii is small in area, but it has some towering peaks. The tallest, Mauna Kea, is 13,796 feet above sea level. Mauna Loa rises to 13,680 feet.

(52)

What is the Great Basin?

Between the Rocky Mountains and the Sierra Nevada-Cascades, there is a region of high plateaus and scattered mountain ranges. Much of this region is so dry that it is desert country, or nearly so. The central part, called the Great Basin, is famous as a land of interior drainage. This means that the waters of most of its rivers and streams do not eventually reach the sea, as the waters of rivers usually do. Instead they flow into salty lakes or disappear into low places in the desert called sinks. The part north of the Great Basin is called the Columbia Plateau, and the part to the south is called the Colorado Plateaus.

What is Death Valley?

This is a deep desert valley in eastern California, near the Nevada border. It contains the lowest and the hottest places in the United States. It gained its name in 1849, when a group of gold seekers started across it, believing it to be a shortcut to the goldfields in the Sierra Nevada. Soon they were overcome by thirst and hunger, and they struggled frantically to find their way out. Only one person died, but the others thought of it as a valley of death.

Which parts of the United States have been built by volcanoes?

All the islands of Hawaii are the tops of volcanic mountains. The Sierra Nevada, the Cascade Range, and the Columbia Plateau are of volcanic origin. So are the peaks of the Aleutian Range in southwestern Alaska.

WONDERS OF THE FIFTY STATES

What is the greatest natural wonder in the fifty states?

Many people would say that the Grand Canyon of the Colorado River, in northern Arizona, is the most impressive and awe-inspiring. It is more than 200 miles long, from 4 to 18 miles wide, and at one point more than a mile deep. The most spectacular parts are included in Grand Canyon National Park and Grand Canyon National Monument.

What is Old Faithful?

It is one of many geysers (springs that spout hot water and steam, not steadily but from time to time) in Yellowstone National Park. Old Faithful is so named because it erupts faithfully about every sixty minutes. Yellowstone National Park, which is mainly in Wyoming, with parts in Idaho and Montana, was the nation's first national park (established in 1872).

Where might you see a volcano erupt?

Kilauea Crater in Hawaii Volcanoes National Park, on the island of Hawaii, provides spectacular fireworks occasionally.

Looking down into the fire pit of Kilauea Crater, an active volcano in Hawaii. (U.S. ARMY AIR CORPS PHOTO FROM CUSHING)

And where could you see glaciers?

Southern Alaska has many large glaciers. The largest, Malaspina Glacier, covers an area about the size of Rhode Island. Two national areas where visitors may see glaciers are Glacier Bay National Monument in Alaska and Glacier National Park in Montana.

Would you prefer the wonders of the seashore or perhaps of forested mountains, sparkling lakes, or wild rivers?

Wonders of these kinds and many more can be seen in areas that have been carefully planned by the National Park Service (of the United States Department of the Interior). There are more than 250 of these areas throughout the fifty states, and the number is ever growing. They are classified according to kinds, such as national parks, national seashores, national recreation areas (around huge man-made lakes), and national wild rivers. Besides natural wonders, there are many man-made wonders (such as prehistoric Indian ruins) and many historical places among the national areas in the fifty states.

And that is not all. The United States Forest Service (of the Department of Agriculture) cares for more than 150 national forests throughout the fifty states. In the forests there are many places where people may camp, hike, hunt, fish, and ski.

Are all the wonders of the fifty states to be found in national parks or forests?

By no means. Every state has a system of state areas, classified in various ways, such as parks, monuments and his-

The Grand Canyon, one of the best-known points of interest in the United States. (AMERICAN AIRLINES)

toric places, beaches, forests, recreation areas, waysides, and parkways. The total number in all of the states exceeds 2,500, and the number grows each year.

Do you know something (or maybe quite a bit) about state systems of parks, forests, and other areas — and about the national system, too?

It is really very easy to get such information. For example, the department of parks in almost every state has available folders and bulletins telling about both state and national areas. State highway departments issue colorful maps showing where these places are and how to reach them.

Indian cliff dwellings in Mesa Verde National Park in Colorado. (CHARLES PHELPS CUSHING)

THE STATES AS PRODUCERS OF GOODS

When we think of what the states produce, we usually think of three main kinds of goods — agricultural (or farm) products, minerals, and manufactured products. Each state produces a share of each of these. But some states are known especially for farm products, others for minerals or for manufacturing, and still others rank high in more than one kind of goods.

Which states rank highest in total value of all farm products sold during a year?

In recent years, California, Iowa, Illinois, and Texas have ranked highest.

Which states are the leaders in total value of all the minerals that they produce?

Usually the leaders are Texas, Louisiana, and California.

And which in manufacturing?

New York, California, Ohio, Pennsylvania, Michigan, and New Jersey have ranked highest in recent times.

How can you find out how much each state produces and where it ranks?

Facts and figures about what a state produces, how much, and where it ranks — like population figures — change from year to year. To find the latest official statistics (facts and figures), look in *The Statistical Abstract of the United States*.* Other handy sources of the latest information are almanacs, such as *The World Almanac and Book of Facts*.

---

*A "statistical abstract" is a summary of facts and figures. Various departments of the United States Government gather so many different kinds of information that all the facts

Of all the farm products of the fifty states, which ones usually rank highest in value?

The value of all the cattle sold is usually higher than the value of any other product. Next come dairy products (milk, butter, and cheese), hogs, corn, soybeans, and wheat. Cattle are the single most valuable product of at least twenty states. In about twenty more states, dairy products rank first or second in value.

Which are the leading corn-growing states?

Illinois, Iowa, and Indiana are usually the leaders.

Which ones are the chief cotton growers?

Texas, Mississippi, California, and Arkansas have been the leaders in recent times.

Which states are famous for potatoes?

Idaho and Maine.

Of all the mineral products of the fifty states, which product usually ranks highest in value?

Petroleum. The leading oil-producing states are Texas, Louisiana, California, and Oklahoma.

Where was the first commercial oil well in the United States?

The first was the Drake well at Titusville, Pennsylvania, in 1859.

---

and figures for just one year fill many books. To give people a handy summary of the kinds of information that they are most likely to want, the Bureau of the Census of the U.S. Department of Commerce publishes the *Statistical Abstract* each year. Most libraries have copies of this important and useful book. It contains information (mostly in the form of tables) about almost anything you could think of — population, health, education, area (and geography and climate), public lands, travel, transportation, science (and space flights and programs), forests, fisheries, agriculture, mining, manufacturing, and much more.

The first oil well in the United States (left), at Titusville, Pennsylvania. (CULVER PICTURES, INC.) Mining for gold (right), about 1900, in Colorado, a state where gold deposits first attracted settlers. (U.S. FOREST SERVICE)

Where were the first gold mines in the United States?

Gold nuggets were found in North Carolina about the year 1800. Georgia had a "gold rush" beginning in 1828.

Which states received their first rush of settlers as a result of gold discoveries?

Those states are Alaska, California, Colorado, Idaho, Montana, Nevada, and South Dakota.

Which state once had diamond mines?

Arkansas. Diamonds were discovered near Murfreesboro in 1906, and the mines there were the only true diamond mines ever found in the United States (or in North Amer-

(60)

ica). The mines are no longer in operation, but many people go to the old mining area and spend hours searching for diamonds.

What kinds of manufactured products rank highest in value?

As you might expect, one of the highest is the kind called "transportation equipment" (cars and trucks, aircraft of all kinds, ships and boats, railroad cars). Other manufactured products that rank high are foods (all the canned, frozen, and packaged foods that you see in supermarkets), electrical machinery (radio and television sets, household appliances, and the like), and nonelectrical machinery (machinery for farms, road building and other construction, offices, and many other uses).

Efficiently run assembly lines help to make automobiles a major product of the United States. (UNITED PRESS INTERNATIONAL)

WHICH STATES CLAIM PRESIDENTS?

Which state is called the "Mother of Presidents"?

VIRGINIA, because more Presidents of the United States have been born there than in any other state. These eight Presidents were born in Virginia (the number following each name tells which President the person was in numerical order):

George Washington, 1st   William Henry Harrison, 9th
Thomas Jefferson, 3rd   John Tyler, 10th
James Madison, 4th   Zachary Taylor, 12th
James Monroe, 5th   Woodrow Wilson, 28th

Which state ranks next in number of Presidents born in the state?

OHIO is a close second, with these seven Presidents:

Ulysses S. Grant, 18th   William McKinley, 25th
Rutherford B. Hayes, 19th   William Howard Taft, 27th
James A. Garfield, 20th   Warren G. Harding, 29th
Benjamin Harrison, 23rd

Which state ranks third?

NEW YORK, which was the birthplace of these four Presidents:

Martin Van Buren, 8th   Theodore Roosevelt, 26th
Millard Fillmore, 13th   Franklin D. Roosevelt, 32nd

Which state is next?

MASSACHUSETTS, with three Presidents:

John Adams, 2nd   John F. Kennedy, 35th
John Quincy Adams, 6th

Which states have been the birthplace of two Presidents each?

NORTH CAROLINA: James K. Polk, 11th
Andrew Johnson, 17th
TEXAS: Dwight D. Eisenhower, 34th
Lyndon B. Johnson, 36th
VERMONT: Chester A. Arthur, 21st
Calvin Coolidge, 30th

Which states claim one President each?

CALIFORNIA: Richard M. Nixon, 37th
IOWA: Herbert Hoover, 31st
KENTUCKY: Abraham Lincoln, 16th
MISSOURI: Harry S Truman, 33rd
NEW HAMPSHIRE: Franklin Pierce, 14th
NEW JERSEY: Grover Cleveland, 22nd and 24th
PENNSYLVANIA: James Buchanan, 15th
SOUTH CAROLINA: Andrew Jackson, 7th

Which state besides South Carolina claims President Jackson? Andrew Jackson was born in Waxhaw, a backwoods settlement on the border between South Carolina and North Carolina, and both states claim the site of the settlement. President Jackson himself considered South Carolina to be his birthplace.

Which states can claim Presidents because those states were the official places of residence of the persons when they were elected President?

The number of states that claim Presidents by reason of residence at the time of their election is about the same as

the number that claim Presidents by reason of birth. But
the list is somewhat different, as you can see:

CALIFORNIA: Herbert Hoover
ILLINOIS: Abraham Lincoln, Ulysses S. Grant
INDIANA: Benjamin Harrison
LOUISIANA: Zachary Taylor
MASSACHUSETTS: John Adams   Calvin Coolidge
        John Quincy Adams John F. Kennedy
MISSOURI: Harry S Truman
NEW HAMPSHIRE: Franklin Pierce
NEW JERSEY: Woodrow Wilson
NEW YORK: Martin Van Buren Theodore Roosevelt
     Millard Fillmore   Franklin D. Roosevelt
     Chester A. Arthur   Dwight D. Eisenhower
     Grover Cleveland   Richard M. Nixon
OHIO: William Henry Harrison William McKinley
   Rutherford B. Hayes William Howard Taft
   James A. Garfield   Warren G. Harding
PENNSYLVANIA: James Buchanan
TENNESSEE: Andrew Jackson Andrew Johnson
     James K. Polk
TEXAS: Lyndon B. Johnson
VIRGINIA: George Washington James Monroe
    Thomas Jefferson   John Tyler
    James Madison

WHICH STATES CLAIM VICE-PRESIDENTS?

As a birthplace of Vice-Presidents of the United States, New York is the leader by far, with eight. Kentucky is next, followed by Ohio and Vermont.

In the following list, the number following the name tells which Vice-President the person was in numerical order. The name of the person who was President at the time is shown in parentheses.

CALIFORNIA: Richard M. Nixon, 36th (Eisenhower)

INDIANA: Thomas R. Marshall, 28th (Wilson)

IOWA: Henry A. Wallace, 33rd (F. D. Roosevelt)

KANSAS: Charles Curtis, 31st (Hoover)

KENTUCKY: Richard M. Johnson, 9th (Van Buren)
John C. Breckinridge, 14th (Buchanan)
Adlai E. Stevenson, 23rd (Cleveland)
Alben W. Barkley, 35th (Truman)

MAINE: Hannibal Hamlin, 15th (Lincoln)

MARYLAND: Spiro Agnew, 39th (Nixon)

MASSACHUSETTS: John Adams, 1st (Washington)
Elbridge Gerry, 5th (Madison)

MISSOURI: Harry S Truman, 34th (F. D. Roosevelt)

NEW HAMPSHIRE: Henry Wilson, 18th (Grant)

NEW JERSEY: Aaron Burr, 3rd (Jefferson)
Garret A. Hobart, 24th (McKinley)

NEW YORK: George Clinton, 4th (Jefferson and Madison)
Daniel D. Tompkins, 6th (Monroe)
Martin Van Buren, 8th (Jackson)
Millard Fillmore, 12th (Taylor)
Schuyler Colfax, 17th (Grant)
William A. Wheeler, 19th (Hayes)

Theodore Roosevelt, 25th (McKinley)

James S. Sherman, 27th (Taft)

NORTH CAROLINA: William R. King, 13th (Pierce)

Andrew Johnson, 16th (Lincoln)

OHIO: Thomas A. Hendricks, 21st (Cleveland)

Charles W. Fairbanks, 26th (T. Roosevelt)

Charles G. Dawes, 30th (Coolidge)

PENNSYLVANIA: George M. Dallas, 11th (Polk)

SOUTH CAROLINA: John C. Calhoun, 7th (John Q. Adams
and Andrew Jackson)

SOUTH DAKOTA: Hubert H. Humphrey, 38th (L. B. Johnson)

TEXAS: John N. Garner, 32nd (F. D. Roosevelt)

Lyndon B. Johnson, 37th (Kennedy)

VERMONT: Chester A. Arthur, 20th (Garfield)

Levi P. Morton, 22nd (B. Harrison)

Calvin Coolidge, 29th (Harding)

VIRGINIA: Thomas Jefferson, 2nd (John Adams)

John Tyler, 10th (W. H. Harrison)

FROM ALABAMIAN TO WYOMINGITE

Are you an Alaskan — or maybe a Marylander, or a Wyoming-ite?

You are one of these, if you live in Alaska, Maryland, or Wyoming. Words such as these make handy names meaning "one who is of — belongs to, or is a resident of" a certain state. You can see how such names are made. A suffix (*-an,* or *-ian*; *-er;* or *-ite*) is simply added to the state name. The following list shows the names the dictionary gives for residents of 48 of the states:

Alabamian; *also* Alabaman
Alaskan
Arizonan; *also* Arizonian
Arkansan; *also* Arkansian *and*
    Arkansawyer
Californian
Coloradan *or* Coloradoan
Connecticuter
Delawarean *or* Delawarian
Floridian *or* Floridan
Georgian
Idahoan
Illinoisan; *also* Illinoisian *or* Illinoian
Indianan *or* Indianian
Iowan
Kansan
Kentuckian
Louisianian; *also* Louisianan
Mainer
Marylander

Michigander *or* Michiganian *or*
    Michiganite
Minnesotan; *also* Minnesotian
Mississippian
Missourian
Montanan *or* Montanian
Nebraskan; *also* Nebraskian
Nevadan; *also* Nevadian
New Hampshireman *or* New Hamp-
    shirite
New Jerseyite
New Mexican
New Yorker
North Carolinian
North Dakotan
Ohioan
Oklahoman
Oregonian
Pennsylvanian
Rhode Islander

South Carolinian Virginian
South Dakotan Washingtonian
Tennessean *or* Tennesseean West Virginian
Texan Wisconsinite
Utahan; *also* Utahn Wyomingite
Vermonter *or* Vermontese

Why is there no name for the people of Hawaii or Massachusetts?

There is a name Hawaiian, but it belongs only to persons of Hawaiian or part-Hawaiian ancestry. As for Massachusetts — anything added to that long state name would make a great mouthful to say! But there is a name for the people of Massachusetts, and that is Bay Staters — made from Massachusetts' nickname, the Bay State.

WHAT'S IN A NICKNAME?

Who's a Hoosier?

A Hoosier is an Indianan. This is the nickname of both the state and the people. No one knows exactly where this name came from or how Indiana acquired it, but it is one of the best known and best loved of all the state nicknames.

Which state is the Show-Me State?

That's Missouri. Although no one knows the exact origin of this nickname, either, almost everyone knows the saying, "I'm from Missouri, and you'll have to show me."

Who are Tarheels?

The people of North Carolina have this nickname, and the state is called the Tarheel State. Tar once was an important product of North Carolina's vast pine forests, but the exact origin of the nickname is uncertain. One story of the origin goes back to the time of the Civil War, 1861–65, when there was talk of putting tar on the heels of some soldiers to make them stick better in battle.

...and Sooners?

They are Oklahomans, and the state is called the Sooner State. This nickname comes from the time (April 22, 1889) when a small amount of land in Oklahoma, then called Indian Territory, was first opened to settlers. People who wanted to claim land were supposed to line up at the border, await the opening signal, and then rush in to stake their claims. But some people had found ways to locate desirable land in advance, and they were able to stake

(69)

their claims "sooner" than the others. They were called "Sooners," and from them the state and the people of Oklahoma acquired a nickname.

Which state is the Volunteer State?

Tennessee proudly bears this nickname. Soldiers from Tennessee, led by Andrew Jackson, played an important part in the War of 1812. Later, during the Mexican War (1846–48), thousands of Tennesseans offered their services. All these volunteers helped to give the state its nickname.

Why is Colorado called the Centennial State?

Colorado's nickname comes from the fact that the state was admitted to the Union in 1876 — the centennial (100th anniversary) of the signing of the Declaration of Independence.

Why is Kentucky called the Bluegrass State?

Kentucky is famous for a kind of grass called bluegrass. It is not really blue, but it has a bluish tinge when it is in full bloom. Some of the world's best-known racehorses have grazed on the bluegrass pastures around Lexington and Louisville.

Which state is the Granite State?

New Hampshire has this nickname, which comes from the fine building granite quarried in the state.

...and the Equality State?

Wyoming well deserves this nickname because in 1869 the Wyoming territorial legislature gave women equal rights with men to vote and hold public office. These rights were included in the state constitution of 1890, making Wyoming the first state in the Union to give women the right to vote.

All the other states have nicknames, too. Some have more than one, and some have had several during their histories. The present nicknames of the rest of the states are given in the following list. Many of these are official — that is, they have been adopted by acts of the state legislatures.

ALABAMA: Yellowhammer State
ALASKA: The Great Land
ARIZONA: Grand Canyon State
ARKANSAS: Land of Opportunity
CALIFORNIA: Golden State
CONNECTICUT: Constitution State
DELAWARE: First State; Diamond State
FLORIDA: Sunshine State
GEORGIA: Empire State of the South; Peach State
HAWAII: Aloha State
IDAHO: Gem State
ILLINOIS: Land of Lincoln
IOWA: Hawkeye State
KANSAS: Sunflower State
LOUISIANA: Pelican State
MAINE: Pine Tree State
MARYLAND: Old Line State
MASSACHUSETTS: Bay State
MICHIGAN: Wolverine State; Water–Winter Wonderland
MINNESOTA: North Star State; Gopher State
MISSISSIPPI: Magnolia State
MONTANA: Treasure State
NEBRASKA: Cornhusker State

NEVADA: Silver State
NEW JERSEY: Garden State
NEW MEXICO: Land of Enchantment
NEW YORK: Empire State
NORTH DAKOTA: Flickertail State
OHIO: Buckeye State
OREGON: Beaver State
PENNSYLVANIA: Keystone State
RHODE ISLAND: Little Rhody
SOUTH CAROLINA: Palmetto State
SOUTH DAKOTA: Coyote State; Sunshine State
TEXAS: Lone Star State
UTAH: Beehive State
VERMONT: Green Mountain State
VIRGINIA: Old Dominion
WASHINGTON: Evergreen State
WEST VIRGINIA: Mountain State
WISCONSIN: Badger State

THE EMBLEMS OF THE STATES

Why do the states have flags, seals, birds, flowers, trees, and other emblems?

One definition of the word *state* is "a body of people politically organized and occupying a certain territory." We can see how this definition applies to a state of the United States. A state, first of all, must have people (there could hardly be a state without people). Then the people must have a certain area of land that they call their own, and they must have a government under which they live.

The people who help to establish, or found, a state are often called "founding fathers." One of the first things they do is to choose a name for the state. The name establishes the identity of the state and helps to give it a "personality."

Then the founders have a flag made, using colors and designs that have a special meaning for the state. The flag becomes the main emblem of the state. Usually the founders choose a motto — a word, phrase, or sentence (often in Latin) that helps express the "character" of the state and

The state flag of New Mexico (left) and the state seal of Kentucky.

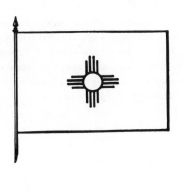

gives the people a principle, or important idea, to guide their lives.

The founders usually give careful thought to the design of at least one other emblem — the state seal, often called the "great seal." The seal becomes the "signature" of the state, and it is placed on all official documents.*

Besides a flag, seal, and motto, each state has a bird, flower, tree, and maybe other emblems that help express the "personality" of the state and tell something important or unusual about it. Sometimes these are chosen early in the life of the state, and sometimes they are selected later. Most of the emblems are official — that is, they have been adopted by acts of the state legislature. In many instances, the schoolchildren of a state have helped to choose the bird, flower, or tree.

The state birds, flowers, and trees are listed on pages 76 and 77. Here are some questions that show how interesting a study of state emblems can be:

Which states have a horse as their state animal?

The Morgan horse is the state animal of Vermont. (The story of the famous Morgan horse is told in the book *Justin*

---

*It would take many pages to show and explain the details of all the flags and seals of the fifty states. The design of almost every one makes an interesting story that tells much about the history and the traditions of the state. The articles on the states in *The New Book of Knowledge* and some other encyclopedias give information about the state emblems. Too, most states have special leaflets or booklets showing and explaining their emblems. These can be obtained by writing to the secretary of state in each state.

(74)

Morgan Had a Horse, by Marguerite Henry.) The Tennessee walking horse is the state animal of Tennessee.

Which states have a dog?

Maryland has the Chesapeake Bay retriever as its state animal. Pennsylvania has the Great Dane, and Virginia, the American foxhound.

What are some of the other state animals?

California: grizzly bear   New Mexico: black bear
Colorado: bighorn sheep   North Dakota: flickertail
Kansas: buffalo   Oregon: beaver
Michigan: wolverine   South Dakota: coyote
Minnesota: gopher   Wisconsin: badger

What are some of the state fish?

Alabama: tarpon   Massachusetts: cod
Alaska: king salmon   Michigan: trout
Maryland: striped bass   New Mexico: cutthroat trout

Which state has a breed of poultry as its state bird?

Rhode Island's state bird is the Rhode Island Red, a breed of poultry developed in the state and known all over the country.

Which state has a goose as its state bird?

The state bird of Hawaii is the nene, or Hawaiian goose.

What is unusual about Delaware's state bird?

The story of Delaware's state bird, the blue hen chicken, goes back to Revolutionary War times. It is said that when a company of Delaware men went off to war, they took with them game chickens (fighting cocks) that were

(75)

of the brood of a famous blue hen. When the men were not in battle, they entertained themselves by holding cockfights. When they were in battle, they fought so well that they were compared to their fighting cocks, and they gained the nickname "Blue Hen's Chickens." Later, Delaware adopted the blue hen chicken as its state bird.

State	Bird	Flower	Tree
Alabama	Yellowhammer	Camellia	Longleaf pine
Alaska	Willow ptarmigan	Forget-me-not	Sitka spruce
Arizona	Cactus wren	Saguaro cactus blossom	Paloverde
Arkansas	Mockingbird	Apple blossom	Shortleaf pine
California	California valley quail	Golden poppy	California redwood
Colorado	Lark bunting	Rocky Mountain columbine	Colorado blue spruce
Connecticut	American robin	Mountain laurel	White oak
Delaware	Blue hen chicken	Peach blossom	American holly
Florida	Mockingbird	Orange blossom	Cabbage palmetto
Georgia	Brown thrasher	Cherokee rose	Live oak
Hawaii	Nene (Hawaiian goose)	Red hibiscus	Kukui (candlenut tree)
Idaho	Mountain bluebird	Syringa	Western white pine
Illinois	Eastern cardinal	Meadow violet	Oak
Indiana	Cardinal	Peony	Tulip tree
Iowa	Eastern goldfinch	Wild rose	Oak
Kansas	Western meadowlark	Sunflower	Cottonwood
Kentucky	Cardinal	Goldenrod	Yellow poplar
Louisiana	Eastern brown pelican	Magnolia	———
Maine	Chickadee	Eastern white pine cone and tassel	Eastern white pine
Maryland	Baltimore oriole	Black-eyed Susan	The Wye Oak
Massachusetts	Chickadee	Mayflower	American elm
Michigan	Robin	Apple blossom	Eastern white pine
Minnesota	Loon	Showy (pink-and-white) lady's slipper	Red (Norway) pine
Mississippi	Mockingbird	Magnolia blossom	Southern magnolia
Missouri	Bluebird	Hawthorn	Flowering dogwood
Montana	Western meadowlark	Bitterroot	Ponderosa pine
Nebraska	Western meadowlark	Goldenrod	American elm

(76)

State	Bird	Flower	Tree
Nevada	Mountain bluebird	Sagebrush	Single-leaf pinyon
New Hampshire	Purple finch	Purple lilac	Paper birch
New Jersey	Eastern goldfinch	Purple violet	Red oak
New Mexico	Roadrunner	Yucca	Pinyon
New York	Bluebird (not official)	Rose	Sugar maple
North Carolina	Cardinal	Dogwood	Pine
North Dakota	Western meadowlark	Wild prairie rose	American elm
Ohio	Cardinal	Scarlet carnation	Ohio buckeye
Oklahoma	Scissor-tailed flycatcher	Mistletoe	Redbud
Oregon	Western meadowlark	Oregon grape	Douglas fir
Pennsylvania	Ruffed grouse	Mountain laurel	Eastern hemlock
Rhode Island	Rhode Island Red	Violet	Maple
South Carolina	Carolina wren	Yellow jessamine	Palmetto
South Dakota	Ring-necked pheasant	Pasqueflower	White spruce
Tennessee	Mockingbird	Iris	Yellow poplar
Texas	Mockingbird	Bluebonnet	Pecan
Utah	California gull	Sego lily	Blue spruce
Vermont	Hermit thrush	Red clover	Sugar maple
Virginia	Cardinal	Flowering dogwood	———
Washington	Willow goldfinch	Coast rhododendron	Western hemlock
West Virginia	Cardinal	Great rhododendron	Sugar maple
Wisconsin	Robin	Violet	Sugar maple
Wyoming	Western meadowlark	Indian paintbrush	Cottonwood

The bluebird (left), the violet (center), and the leaf and acorn of the white oak (right). Can you find the states to which each of these belongs?

ABBREVIATIONS OF STATE NAMES

Just as we do not spell words in any way that pops into our heads, so we do not abbreviate words in just any fashion. We use *standard spellings and abbreviations* (the spellings and abbreviations given in the dictionary). The following are the standard abbreviations of the state names. Where two abbreviations are given, the first one is preferred. A black line means "Do not abbreviate."

ALABAMA: Ala.
ALASKA: —
ARIZONA: Ariz.
ARKANSAS: Ark.
CALIFORNIA: Calif.; Cal.
COLORADO: Colo.
CONNECTICUT: Conn.
DELAWARE: Del.
FLORIDA: Fla.
GEORGIA: Ga.
HAWAII: —
IDAHO: —
ILLINOIS: Ill.
INDIANA: Ind.
IOWA: —
KANSAS: Kans.
KENTUCKY: Ky.
LOUISIANA: La.
MAINE: Me.
MARYLAND: Md.
MASSACHUSETTS: Mass.
MICHIGAN: Mich.
MINNESOTA: Minn.
MISSISSIPPI: Miss.
MISSOURI: Mo.

MONTANA: Mont.
NEBRASKA: Nebr.; Neb.
NEVADA: Nev.
NEW HAMPSHIRE: N.H.
NEW JERSEY: N.J.
NEW MEXICO: N.Mex.; N.M.
NEW YORK: N.Y.
NORTH CAROLINA: N.C.
NORTH DAKOTA: N.Dak.; N.D.
OHIO: —
OKLAHOMA: Okla.
OREGON: Oreg.; Ore.
PENNSYLVANIA: Pa.
RHODE ISLAND: R.I.
SOUTH CAROLINA: S.C.
SOUTH DAKOTA: S.Dak.; S.D.
TENNESSEE: Tenn.
TEXAS: Tex.
UTAH: —
VERMONT: Vt.
VIRGINIA: Va.
WASHINGTON: Wash.
WEST VIRGINIA: W.Va.
WISCONSIN: Wis.; Wisc.
WYOMING: Wyo.

THE STATES AND THEIR CAPITALS — A LIST

Here are lists that you can use to test yourself or someone else on naming the state capitals. If you are testing yourself, cover the capitals with a strip of paper.

State	Capital
1. Alabama	1. Montgomery
2. Alaska	2. Juneau
3. Arizona	3. Phoenix
4. Arkansas	4. Little Rock
5. California	5. Sacramento
6. Colorado	6. Denver
7. Connecticut	7. Hartford
8. Delaware	8. Dover
9. Florida	9. Tallahassee
10. Georgia	10. Atlanta
11. Hawaii	11. Honolulu
12. Idaho	12. Boise
13. Illinois	13. Springfield
14. Indiana	14. Indianapolis
15. Iowa	15. Des Moines
16. Kansas	16. Topeka
17. Kentucky	17. Frankfort
18. Louisiana	18. Baton Rouge
19. Maine	19. Augusta
20. Maryland	20. Annapolis
21. Massachusetts	21. Boston
22. Michigan	22. Lansing
23. Minnesota	23. Saint Paul

State	Capital
24. Mississippi	24. Jackson
25. Missouri	25. Jefferson City
26. Montana	26. Helena
27. Nebraska	27. Lincoln
28. Nevada	28. Carson City
29. New Hampshire	29. Concord
30. New Jersey	30. Trenton
31. New Mexico	31. Santa Fe
32. New York	32. Albany
33. North Carolina	33. Raleigh
34. North Dakota	34. Bismarck
35. Ohio	35. Columbus
36. Oklahoma	36. Oklahoma City
37. Oregon	37. Salem
38. Pennsylvania	38. Harrisburg
39. Rhode Island	39. Providence
40. South Carolina	40. Columbia
41. South Dakota	41. Pierre
42. Tennessee	42. Nashville
43. Texas	43. Austin
44. Utah	44. Salt Lake City
45. Vermont	45. Montpelier
46. Virginia	46. Richmond
47. Washington	47. Olympia
48. West Virginia	48. Charleston
49. Wisconsin	49. Madison
50. Wyoming	50. Cheyenne

AND JUST FOR FUN — A PUZZLE

Can you find the names of all fifty states? (The names may read up, down, forward, backward, or diagonally.)

INDEX

ABOUT THE AUTHOR

Sue R. Brandt has lived in six of the fifty states—California, Colorado, Illinois, Michigan, Missouri (born there), and New York. She is a graduate of the University of Chicago, has taught school in Missouri, Illinois, and Michigan, and has worked as an editor in both Chicago and New York. Mrs. Brandt was the editor in charge of articles about the fifty states of the United States for the first edition of *The New Book of Knowledge* and is now a member of the editorial staff of the *Encyclopedia Americana*. She is the author of *How To Write a Report*, also published by Franklin Watts, Inc.